PRINT MAKING

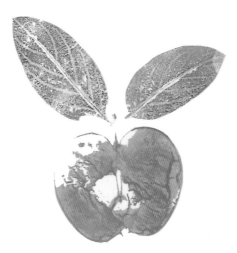

PRINT MAKING

ELISABETH HARDEN

CHARTWELL
BOOKS, INC.

A QUARTO BOOK

Published by
Chartwell Books
A Division of Book Sales, Inc.
PO Box 7100
Edison, New Jersey 08818–7100

This edition produced for sale in the U.S.A., its
territories, and dependencies only.

ISBN 0-7858-0464-1

This book was designed and produced by
Quarto Children's Books Ltd,
The Fitzpatrick Building,
188–194 York Way,
London N7 9QP

Editors Jane Havell and Simon Beecroft
Designer Michael Leaman
Picture researcher Vicky King
Photographer Paul Forester
Indexer Hilary Bird

Creative Director Louise Jervis
Senior Art Editor Nigel Bradley

Many people helped in the creation of this book.
Special thanks must be given to Moira Wills, Eleanor O'Brien, Judy Martin,
Jenevieve Harden, Alec Harden, and Janet White

Quarto would like to thank the following for providing photographs, and for granting permission to reproduce copyright material:
(a = above, b = below, c = center, l = left, r = right)
32bl: ACE Photo Agency/Edmund Nagele; 32br ACE Photo Agency/Mugshots;
54b courtesy of IBM UK Ltd; 72bl The Bridgeman Art Library;
82tr ACE Photo Agency/Alexis Sofianopoulous; 83tr The Bridgeman Art Library;

While every effort has been made to trace and acknowledge all copyright holders,
we would like to apologise should any omissions have been made.

Typeset by Michael Leaman Design Partnership
Manufactured by Bright Arts (Pte) Ltd, Singapore
Printed by C & C (Offset) Ltd, Hong Kong

Contents

Introduction	10	The four seasons	52
Materials and methods	12	Cameras and computers	54
Printing myself	14	Monoprints	56
Potato butterflies	16	Multicolored monoprints	58
Fruit and vegetable prints	18	Lino cuts	60
Trying other materials	20	Colored lino cuts	62
Plain or stripy	22	Lino cut experiments	64
Bits and pieces	24	Signed and sealed	66
Printing nature	26	Lasting impressions	68
Ferns, feathers, and fronds	28	Rubbings	70
Rubber stamping	30	Etching and scratching	72
Animal footprints	32	Silk-screen printing	74
Coiled string and wire	34	Multicolored screen-printing	76
Printing landscapes	36	Fabric printing	78
Disappearing ink	38	Fancy dress	80
Marbled patterns	40	Lithography	82
Backgrounds and distance	42	Wood works	84
Print the town	44	Living in print	86
Fantastic flowers	46	Printed celebrations	88
Stenciling	48	Finishing work	90
My word!	50	Index	92

Introduction

PRINTING IS FUN. YOU CAN make extraordinary shapes and textures from the most ordinary things, and repeat a pattern lots of times within a few minutes. You can decorate boldly, quickly, and cheaply, and let your imagination run riot to make beautiful pictures.

THE PRINTING PRESS

This book would not exist without the invention of the printing press. This machine reproduces text repeatedly by pressing the ink from movable letter molds, called typefaces. Before this, manuscripts (meaning "written by hand") were made individually. Only the very rich could afford them. Print was one of the most important inventions in history, because it made the knowledge contained in books available to millions of ordinary people. Now it is all done by computers, and it's faster still!

◀ An old-fashioned printing press, operated by a hand lever. It was hard work!

◀ An intricately decorated capital C, painted by hand to adorn a medieval manuscript.

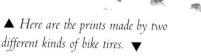

▲ Here are the prints made by two different kinds of bike tires. ▼

▲ A paw print from your pet might look like this!

Any repeated pattern made by pressing
something down onto a surface, or rolling it
along, so that marks come off it over and over
again, is printing. You've probably done it by
accident lots of times!

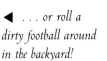

▶ *Here's what happens
if you walk on a clean
floor with your muddy
trainers . . .*

◀ *. . . or roll a
dirty football around
in the backyard!*

▼ *Rubber tires come
in lots of interesting
patterns.*

JAPANESE WOOD-CUT PRINTS

Some of the very best prints were
made in Japan in the 18th and
19th centuries. Japanese artists
were inspired by the landscape –
particularly mountains and
oceans. Hokusai, who produced
this mountain scene, is the most
famous. He often used as many as
90 separate wood blocks to make
his highly colorful, detailed prints.

Materials and methods

Here are some of the things you will need to make prints. Most materials are very simple and cheap. The most useful of all is a box full of bits and pieces, scraps, and oddments which you can use to make wonderful shapes and textures. You will find lots of suggestions throughout the book. Printing can be a messy business, so it is important to have a large clear surface, plenty of newspaper, rags, and overalls. Then, with a few paints and some paper, you are ready to start!

▲ *You ink a roller by dotting printing ink onto a large smooth surface, such as Formica or glass, then passing the roller up and down a few times. This transfers the ink to the roller, which you can then roll quickly over a sheet of paper.*

PAPERS

As well as newspaper, which is a must, it is worth collecting different kinds of paper to experiment with. Drawing paper is essential, but blotting paper, tissue paper, and wrapping paper are also good. Keep plenty of scrap paper to try things out, too.

Stencil paper

Blotting paper

Drawing paper

Corrugated cardboard

Wrapping paper

Card

Lino

PRINTING TOOLS

You will need a paint brush, glue brush, and toothbrush (for spattering paint). Some of the prints in this book were made by brushing paint directly onto a printing block, some by using other things like sponges or cardboard to make the marks. Other prints were made using a roller and an inked slab. This method gives a smoother layer of paint and is very easy.

Brushes

Pencils

Felt tips

Sponges

Scissors

Craft knife

Roller

BURNISHING

To make a really clear print, you need to press the ink evenly right into the paper. This can be done with the back of a wooden spoon and is called burnishing. You could also use a clean roller on top of a sheet of clean paper. All professional printmakers are very clean and tidy and have places for everything. They are also very good at clearing up! Look at page 91 for how to organise things, and tips for drying and storing your finished work.

Poster paint

P.V.A. adhesive

PAINTS AND INKS

Poster paint, either on its own or diluted with water, is fine for some printing, and you can make a huge range of colors by mixing. Many of the prints in the book are made with water-based printing inks, which work well with a roller. Some methods — such as marbling, screen printing, and fabric printing — require special inks and these will be described later.

SAFETY NOTE

You will be using things that need handling with care. Paints are messy, bleach can do damage, and blades and sharp points can hurt you. So be very, very careful, and keep a few sticking plasters nearby.

Water-based printing inks

Printing myself

Y OU HAVE READY-MADE printing equipment at your fingertips – literally! A fingerprint is your very own mark: no one else has exactly the same pattern of whorls and circles. Many crimes are solved through police discovering tell-tale fingerprints, and footprints sometimes give the game away as well. There are other parts of the body that print in distinctive ways and make interesting patterns, too.

FINGERPRINTS

Roll a thin film of printing ink onto a slab. Get your friends to press their fingers and thumbs in the ink and then onto a sheet of paper. If you look at these prints through a magnifying glass you will see that no two are the same.

It's easy to recognize a whole hand, but what about other parts? These creatures are made using fingers and thumbs. You could also experiment with knuckles, fingernails, even hair!

FINGERPRINT BEES

With a few lines added, a fingerprint can become many different creatures. Try a swarm of bees that start as very small dots, then print with your fingertips to make them bigger. Add wings and features with a pen or pencil, then give them a beehive! Try drawing faces on a few prints and see what appears.

14

SHOE PRINTS

Look at the soles of your shoes and see if they have a pattern. Many have ridges and ripples for particular reasons – gripping the ground on a sports field, preventing slipping in icy weather, walking on different surfaces, or just for decoration. How many shoe patterns can you find around the house?

Wrapping paper covered with lip prints.

LIP PRINTS

Lips make wonderful prints. Put on a good thick layer of lipstick – it helps to look in a mirror to get a good shape. Now press your lips firmly onto a sheet of paper. Try making a kiss or a smile and see what happens.

A lip-print Valentine's Day card.

Potato butterflies

MAKING MARKS BY STAMPING an inked surface onto another surface is called relief printing. One of the easiest ways to make a relief print is to press an inked potato shape onto paper. You may have tried this already, and discovered patterns you can make with other simple vegetables. Use a big, even-shaped potato and start by cutting it neatly in half. Let the cut surface dry for about five minutes before you start.

SIMPLE POTATO PRINTS

Using a craft knife, cut a design into the flat surface of one half of a good-sized potato – you could draw it beforehand with a felt-tip pen. Make sure that the potato outside the design is cut well away so that the edges will print cleanly. With a little practice, you can cut more complicated shapes, or you can use a pastry cutter for a ready-made design.

Now lay a piece of flat sponge in a saucer and cover it with paint, allowing it to soak in well. Press the potato block onto this printing pad, and then press it firmly onto a sheet of paper. When you have made several prints, the image will become fainter. Re-ink the block when you need to and then start again.

WHAT YOU NEED

Large potato or swede

Paint

Sponge

Saucers and plates

Thick paint brushes

Kitchen knife and craft knife

Pastry or cookie cutter

Plain paper and newspaper

BETTER PRINTS
• Place newspaper underneath the printing paper.
• Rock the potato slightly so that you make sure that all parts touch the paper.

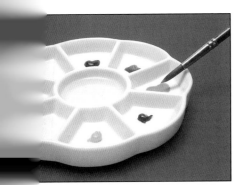

MULTICOLORED BUTTERFLIES

Using different colors on the same block can sometimes produce exciting results. Mix puddles of thick paint in several colors on a palette, or a large plate. Paint these evenly onto different areas of the potato block. Press the block firmly onto the paper.

ANOTHER BUTTERFLY

If you have any paint left, you can make another kind of butterfly. Fold some paper in half and open it out again. Paint some thick blobs of different-colored paint on one side, edging in to the fold mark. Fold the paper again, press it all over evenly, starting from the fold, open it carefully, and — hey presto!

Potato blocks don't last very long. If you want to continue printing later or change the image, slice off the old design and start again on the fresh surface. Other root vegetables, such as the swede or turnip, can make good printing blocks — try them and see which works best.

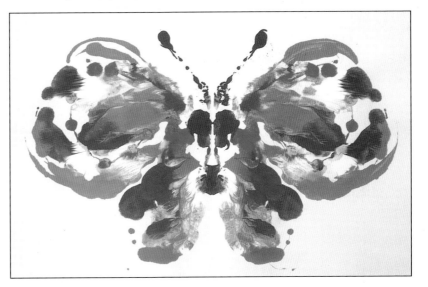

Repeat printing makes paler colors, overlapping blends colors.

◀ *Cutting the block in half down the center of the image will give you a different shape. These resting butterflies are made by cutting the first printing block in half.*

Fruit and vegetable prints

Many fruits and vegetables have patterns of their own, and make wonderful ready-made printing blocks. Artists and designers have used these natural patterns to give them ideas for creating materials such as fabric and wallpapers. Try printing with as many fruits and vegetables as you can find and cut them in different directions. You will have some amazing surprises – and probably a few soggy messes!

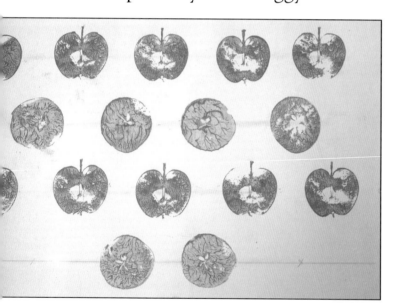

Prints and patterns using an apple

Choose two firm apples, and cut one in half across the middle and the other from top to bottom. If you can find one with a stalk, the pattern will be more interesting. You can either press the fruit onto an inked sponge, or use a roller and printing ink. Take the crosswise-cut apple and press it into the paint or roll it all over with a roller, then press it onto some paper. Now try with the other apple – don't forget the stalk! Can you see the difference between the two prints?

Apple paper

To make regular patterned wrapping paper, draw guidelines over the page with a soft pencil and a ruler. Space dots evenly along the first line, and stagger them on the next line. Print apple prints on the dots. When dry, rub away the pencil marks.

Experiment with fruit and vegetable prints in odd colors.

Canopy of stiff paper
painted with colored stripes.

MAKING A GREENGROCER'S STALL

Here is a chance to show all your prints together. This greengrocer's stall has boxes of fruit in different colors. You could add your own name and advertising on the top.

Grapes hang on
paper ropes.

Rolled-up tubes
for support.

Old shoe boxes, or box
shapes cut from white card,
display the produce.

Prints of apples, potatoes,
and cabbage fill the boxes.

Trying other materials

Y OU CAN MAKE LONGER-lasting printing blocks by gluing objects to thick card. This is called collage, from the French word meaning "to glue." It's a chance to be really inventive and to experiment with lots of different materials and textures. When you arrange the items on the block, remember that to print well they all need to be at about the same level.

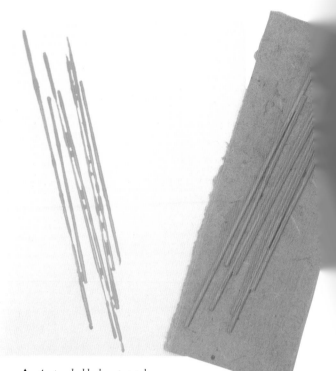

▲ *A simple block print taken from wooden sticks*

WHAT PRINTS WELL?

Paper clips, sandpaper, materials such as lace, buttons, small beads, crumpled sweet papers, chains, dried peas and lentils, rice, pasta.

Let the paint dry before you lift the doily from the paper

PRINTING WITH A PAPER DOILY

Lace-effects and frills can be created quickly and easily using paper doilies.

MAKING A COLLAGE BLOCK

Arrange materials that might print in an interesting way. Remember that the block will print better if the surface is level.

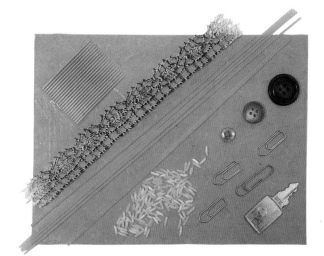

The block print would make a good book cover.

WHAT YOU NEED

Materials to print
Cardboard or hardboard
PVA glue and glue brush
Printing ink or paint
Inking roller or paintbrush
Soft, thin paper for printing

1 Cut a base of strong cardboard or hardboard, and spread it with a layer of glue. Press your materials firmly into the glue. Put a weight on top of the block and let it dry. Paint on a second thin layer of glue.

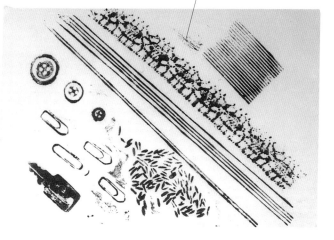

2 Cover your roller with ink and roll it evenly over your block. Place a sheet of paper over the inked block, hold it firmly with one hand, and press it down evenly all over with the other hand, with the back of a spoon, or with a clean, hard roller.

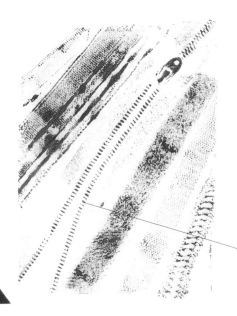

A GLUE BLOCK

You can use glue itself to print. Spread it thickly over some card, and make patterns in it as it dries – you can press small objects into the surface, or create ripples by swirling a comb across it. When the block is dry, print it in the same way as the collage block.

Tapes and ribbons make great textures. The zip makes a railroad track!

PRINTING A STRONGER IMAGE

If you use more pressure to print, you get a stronger picture. The traditional way of increasing pressure is to use a printing press, but you can use heavy weights – such as a garden roller, a mangle, or a large board covered with bricks or stones.

Plain or stripy

THINK BEFORE YOU THROW OLD boxes and wrapping paper into the bin. Some of these materials are perfect ready-made printing blocks, and, with a little experimental cutting and tearing, you can print wonderful pictures from them. Corrugated cardboard has a ridged surface, so all the pattern-making is done for you, but you can cut and arrange it to make more complicated designs.

WHAT YOU NEED

Smooth cardboard cut in the shape of sails
Pieces of thick card
Paint and inking roller or paint brush
Sponge and cotton wool
Old toothbrush and blunt knife

MAKING HANDLES FOR PRINTING BLOCKS

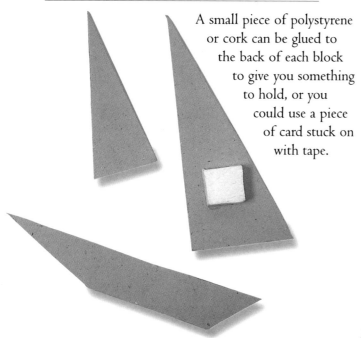

A small piece of polystyrene or cork can be glued to the back of each block to give you something to hold, or you could use a piece of card stuck on with tape.

A GATHERING STORM

Printing blocks can be used again and again to create a range of different pictures. The same triangular shapes are used in the prints below to make boats on a calm sea as well as boats in a terrible storm!

I Paint a bright blue sky and a turquoise sea. Let it dry. Cut cardboard blocks in the shape of four sails of different sizes. Apply white paint with a roller or paintbrush, then press them onto the sea scene as if they were sailing in calm weather.

2 Now the wind is starting to blow and tipping the sails! The sky is painted grayer. The big clouds are printed with cotton wool, and the waves on the dark, churning sea are printed with triangles of ripped cardboard covered with white paint.

UTTING CORRUGATED
ARDBOARD COLLAGES

mouthful of words, but what a mass
of patterns can be made from one
iece of corrugated cardboard! This
rint is made using blocks of
orrugated paper, which have been
rranged so that the lines run in
different directions.

Rolls of corrugated cardboard, printed end on,
make wheels, tank tyres, and cabbages. The
cabbages at the far end of this field are made
from smaller blocks, printed more faintly.

3 *The boats are blown right over in the gale! Dark gray
clouds are printed with a sponge, and white spray is
made by spattering paint from a toothbrush.*

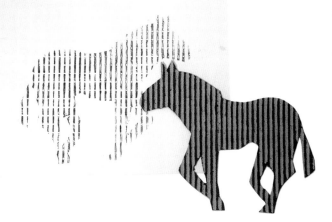

▲ *Draw the shape of a zebra on the back of
a sheet of corrugated cardboard. Cut out the
shape, brush thick paint onto the ridges, lay
your paper on top and press firmly to print.*

23

Bits and pieces

Half the fun of printing is in finding the amazing marks left by quite ordinary objects. Sometimes these are obvious, but some are so strange that you can use them to make a guessing game to puzzle your friends.

BUBBLES IN THE BATH

It's hard to believe you could print from bubbles, but you can! Mix a little dishwashing liquid and water-based paint in a glass. Blow into the bottom through a straw until the bubbles reach the top of the glass. Lay a piece of paper gently over the colored bubbles, then peel it off with great care.

▶ *Try making your bubbles print into a picture by adding a drawing, such as this overflowing bathtub!*

SET OF PUZZLE CARDS

These are some things you could try printing on cards to test your friends — a safety pin, a brush, a key, a fork, a doily, a length of tape. Look around your home to get more ideas. Try pieces of cork or wood, shells, bottle tops, bicycle tyres, and lengths of chain.

◀ *Try to spot which print comes from a sieve or a shoelace.*

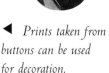

◀ *Prints taken from buttons can be used for decoration.*

24

MAKE A MEAL OF IT

You'll find that you can make some prints that look exactly like things to eat. Try cutting out shapes and using the right colors to make platefuls of paper food! You can have lots of fun getting friends to try and guess what you made your printing blocks from. Can you work out how the baked beans on toast were made, without looking at the caption?

▶ *These prints were made from salad and vegetable leaves, potatoes, and apples.*

Tomatoes made from a cut apple

▲ *These baked beans are printed from bubble wrap and the toast from a sponge.*

◀ *The sausages are printed with fingers, an egg with a potato block, and bacon with scraps of ribbon.*

25

Printing nature

Nature has been printing its own image since time began. Perhaps you've seen the fossilized imprint of a delicate leaf or shell. Making a one-minute print from a leaf will leave a pattern that would take hours to paint with a brush! And remember, each side of a leaf will print a different pattern. A short treasure hunt outdoors could produce a whole collection of things to print — such as leaves, bark, seed pods, and twigs.

Corn stalks

PRINTING LEAVES

Collect leaves with attractive patterns or strongly marked veins, in different shapes and sizes — skeleton leaves are very good. Seed pods and dried flowers have unusual textures. The more things you try, the more surprises you will have!

To take prints, roll some ink over the leaf, then lay your paper on top. Using a clean, dry roller, roll gently and evenly across the paper. Peel the leaf away from the bottom of the paper to see the wonderful pattern you have made.

f prints

► *Leaves are delicate, so you need to take care when printing from them.*

Add insects to make a leaf print look like a tree!

A FRIEZE OF LEAVES

Cover a long surface with newspaper and prepare your inks and rollers. Cut some lengths of lining paper approximately 3ft (1m) long and cut these in half lengthwise so that you have a long strip about 12in (30cm) wide. Lay this out on your surface and put a weight on each end. Lay some leaves on a sheet of newspaper and roll ink over them. Starting at one end of your paper roll, print a pattern of leaves. Use more than one color to make it more interesting.

▼ *You could join several friezes together to go round your room or the top of your bed.*

27

Ferns, feathers, and fronds

SOME THINGS TAKE AN ENORMOUSLY LONG TIME
to draw and paint, and are never quite as good
as the real thing. By printing feathers and ferns, you
can make an instant picture without all the fuss of
tiny lines and thin brushes. With feathers, you'll
need to collect quite a few because the fronds
tend to stick together.

BIRDS IN A BIRDBATH

Feathers make wonderful prints.
Here, they are used to make birds
splashing around in a birdbath and
others in flight. The birdbath is
cut out from paper sponged with
gray paint and spattered with paint
from a toothbrush. Draw the beaks
and feet on later with a felt-tip pen.

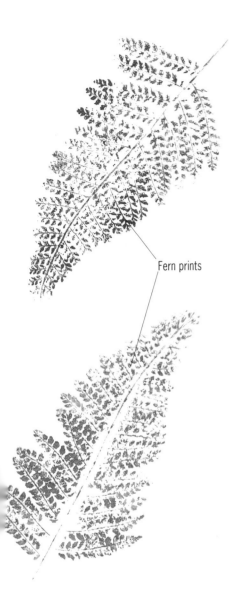

Fern prints

YOUR OWN CARRIER BAG

The easiest way to make a carrier bag is to use a shop one as a pattern. Take it to pieces along the joins, and cut your own paper to the same shape. Or you could glue your own paper onto an existing bag, or – easiest of all – lay a plain bag flat and print straight onto it.

1 *Use ferns to print black and white patterns all over a large sheet of strong brown paper. Each side of a fern will give you a different image.*

2 *When it is dry, cut out the bag shape, and stick the sides together. Tape string handles firmly to the inside of the top edge – folding this over first will make it stronger.*

Fern prints on a carrier bag.

29

Rubber stamping

RUBBER STAMPS ARE THE very best way of stamping images – they give clean, crisp edges, and take a long time to wear out. They are often used to stamp letters and passports and all kinds of documents. Rubber printing sets are quite cheap to buy, but it is more fun to make your own!

▲ *You can buy lovely ready-made rubber stamps like these with quite elaborate patterns. Use food coloring instead of ink, and you can stamp them (gently!) onto iced cookies, but do first make sure the coloring is safe to eat.*

MAKING YOUR OWN

WHAT YOU NEED

Rubber eraser
Fine felt-tip pen
Craft knife
Paints or inks
White and colored papers

Draw a design on the flat surface of a large eraser with a felt-tip pen. Use a craft knife to cut away the rubber around the shape, making sure that you don't cut too much. Try to avoid cutting under your shape, because that will make it less firm. Try it out first on rough paper to see what kind of pattern it makes. You may need to neaten the edges or make the shape simpler. If you have a disaster, don't worry – just slice off the surface and start again!

▶ This brick wall would be great for a dolls' house.

▲ Why not try making your own wallpaper?

◀ *Rubber stamps can be used to print paper for train sets, models, and dolls' houses. This dolls' house floor was made by dipping a rubber stamp in two different colors of paint. The result looks like patterned stone.*

JUMPING FLEAS!

A flick book is a way of making an image seem to move. Cut a tiny flea design into an eraser, and print it on each page of a plain notebook, putting it a little bit higher on each page. When you reach the top, print it coming down. Flick through the pages of the book to make the flea jump up and down! Can you think of any other flick book ideas?

Put images near the edges, so you can flick really fast.

Animal footprints

Have you ever painted a really lovely picture, left it to dry, and found that your dog or cat has walked all over it, leaving muddy footprints? Or have you noticed a slab of newly laid concrete where a dog has left its pawprints? Prints left by animals are very distinctive, and can give you lots of information long after the animal has gone. They also make interesting patterns!

▲ *When marks like this cat's pawprints are made on top of the paper, the print is called positive. The shapes left inside something soft that has been dented, like snow or sand, are called negative prints, or imprints.*

◄ *People use animal imprints in many ways. Hunters sometimes follow game by tracking the marks that animals leave in wet ground, sand, or snow. Native Americans are very skilled at reading tracks. They can tell how many animals are in a group, how fast they are going, and even how long ago they passed.*

▲ *Making imprints with bare feet in the sand is always fun! Try to find smooth, firm sand that is just slightly damp.*

◄ *The horseshoe stamp made from this eraser prints on top of the paper, so it is positive.*

Cover a large box with brown paper, or leave it if there is no printing on it. Make blocks in the shape of different animal paws out of pieces of cardboard – here, we've made the marks of a penguin and a mouse. Print them all over the surface, disappearing beneath the lid. Add others if you like. Then hide some toy animals inside!

Cut-out animals – and their footprints!

Mouse prints made with finger and thumb

Ant prints made with a rubber stamp

Coiled string and wire

STRING IS EASY TO COLLECT. THERE are many different thicknesses and patterns of string, rope, and plastic-covered wire. You can make lots of interesting prints by winding and curling them, either just on their own or first made into a printing block.

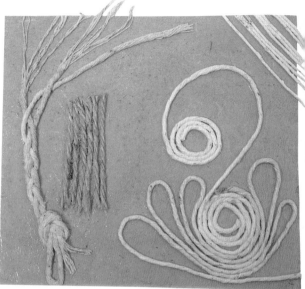

A STRING BLOCK

First choose your string and get it ready – you can use lots of different kinds, or one long piece curled round and round. Cover a cardboard block with plenty of glue, wait until it is tacky, and lay your string on top. String can be springy so you may need to hold it in place. Put a weight on top of the block, and leave it to dry. Put several thick layers of wettish paint on the block – string is very absorbent. Lay a sheet of paper on top of the block, press all over evenly with your fingers or a clean roller, then peel the paper off.

Single lengths of curly string, printed green, make coiled snakes.

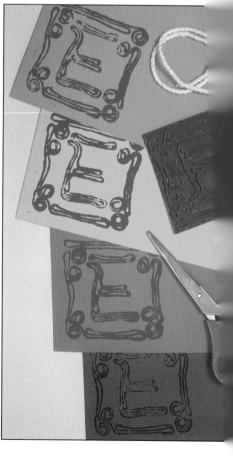

▲ *Pieces of string coiled tightly together make a decorative block to print your own initial. Remember to put on plenty of paint before printing.*

PULLED STRING PRINTS

Fold a piece of paper in half, open it up, and smear some white chalk across the surface. Mix some pools of fairly thick paint and dip a piece of string in each until they are well coated. Lay the strings across the paper with the ends hanging out, and fold the paper again. Holding the paper firmly with one hand, pull the strings out with the other. Inside, you will have printed lovely swirly patterns.

EDIBLE PATTERNS

Bend thick plastic-covered wire into a pattern and glue it onto a block of cardboard the same size as a piece of toast. Remember to write letters the wrong way round (the way they would look in a mirror), so that they will print the right way round. Press the block firmly into a thick slice of bread. Toast the bread, and your pattern will appear as if by magic!

Printing landscapes

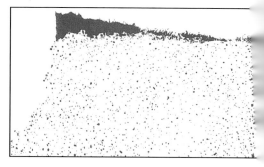

Now you've tried making printed marks with different things, start thinking up ideas about what kind of pictures you would like to print. Try a landscape – either find a real subject outside, or copy from a favorite picture. And, of course, you can always print something from your imagination – such as the Moon's surface or a primeval swamp!

▲ *The rough texture of sandpaper makes excellent cliffs. Print with the rough side for the stony cliff face, and use the smooth side for the grassy clifftop.*

WHAT YOU NEED

Sandpaper, several grades
Cardboard
Paints
Printing inks
Roller
Glue
Celery stick

Add spikes on the cacti with the edge of a piece of card.

The hovering birds were made with a slice of celery.

Use a circle of card for the sun.

GRAND CANYON

Draw a rough outline of your picture on a large sheet of paper, and fill in the sky and distant landscape with paints or crayons. Use paper covered with thick yellow paint to print the clifftop, and different-sized pieces of cardboard for the cliffs.

MAKING THE MOST OF COLORED PAPER

Simple shapes of torn paper and card make very effective printing blocks when you use them on different-colored background papers.

▲ Icebergs floating in a blue sea

Misty mountains in a pale blue sky

▶ Rough rocks in yellow sand

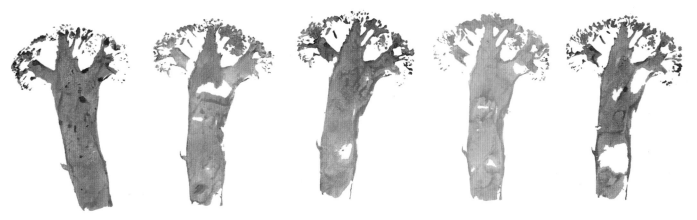

▲ A cauliflower sprig makes a brilliant tree!

Disappearing ink

INSTEAD OF PRINTING COLOR ONTO the paper, you can start by inking the paper and then making the color disappear so that the white paper shows through. This is done with bleach, which can be dangerous so handle it with care and cover yourself up well. Don't let it touch your clothes or any furniture.

Water-soluble ink

Container for bleach

Cork

Bottle tops

Celery

Toothpicks

Brush

Cord

PRINTING WITH BLEACH

Always cover your work surface with plenty of newspaper, and cover yourself with a big overall – bleach can do damage. Paint a layer of water-soluble ink all over a large sheet of paper. While it is drying, rough out a picture on paper – here it is a fish in the sea. You print or draw with bleach instead of paint, which makes the ink disappear.

<table>
<tr><td>WHAT YOU NEED</td></tr>
<tr><td>Overalls</td></tr>
<tr><td>Plenty of newspaper</td></tr>
<tr><td>Printing materials, such as plastic bottle tops, feathers, corks, a piece of celery, old pencils</td></tr>
<tr><td>A saucer containing a little bleach</td></tr>
<tr><td>Water-soluble ink</td></tr>
</table>

The fish scales are printed with celery and a cork.

Make fine lines with a toothpick or twig, dipped in bleach.

The bubbles are printed with bottle tops and the end of a cardboard tube.

MAKING A FRAME

Your pictures will look really good if you frame them. Cut a rectangle of white card so the inside edge is the right size to show your picture, and the outside edge is several inches larger. Paint the card with watered-down or soluble ink, and use bleach to print a pattern on it that matches your picture.

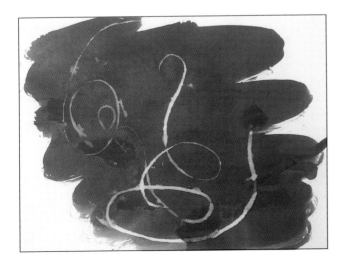

◄ *Experiment with using bleach to take out the colours of other inks and paints.*

SAFETY NOTE
Don't let bleach touch your hands, eyes, or clothes. If it does, wash it off immediately with plenty of cold water.

Marbled patterns

MARBLING IS AN EXCITING PROCESS because you are never quite sure what kind of pattern is going to appear! It works because oil and water don't mix – the oil in the paint stays on the surface of the water, and will stick to the paper when you take a print. The swirly patterns make wonderful backgrounds to print on. Once you've started marbling you won't want to stop.

MARBLED PAPER

1 *Mix your paint in a pot with white spirit until it is runny. Half fill the tin with water. Swirl the paint around on the surface of the water using the end of your paintbrush.*

2 *Lay a sheet of paper very gently on the top of the water, and smooth away any bubbles. Take care not to push the paper under the surface.*

3 *Lift the paper off gently from one end, and lay it flat to dry.*

BETTER MARBLING
Adding a little wallpaper paste to the water makes marbling easier to do.

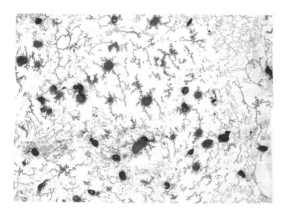

WHAT YOU NEED

Oil paints, or powder paints mixed with cooking oil

White spirit

Paintbrushes

Old yoghurt pots

Old baking tin or tray

Newspaper

GOLDFISH POND

The swirly patterns of marbled paper make a good "water" effect in a picture. Here, it's used for a fish pond, with color prints round the outside for the stone. Paint some orange goldfish in the pond with thick paint. Mix some green paint and paint a few lily leaves overlapping the fish. Then add a watchful cat!

All these papers have been made by marbling. Use sheets of marbling to cover books or folders. With smaller scraps you can make or decorate cards, jewelry, or paper patchworks. You can even marble ribbon.

Backgrounds and distance

Y OU CAN HAVE FUN MAKING SKIES and backgrounds with printing. It is the best and quickest way to paint large areas very quickly. Also, it is very good for making clouds — especially dramatic storm clouds.

Different-sized cabbage leaves are very good for printing trees. Try other leaves as well for a range of effects.

TREES IN THE PARK

A few cabbage leaves, printed onto white paper, then cut out, made nearly every tree in this park! Yellowy-green ink was rolled onto a slab and used for some of the trees. Then, blue ink was added to make mid-green, and more blue to print the darkest trees. The park fence was printed with the edge of a piece of card.

DISTANCE EFFECTS

You can create the feeling of distance very easily with printing, by making things that are far away look faint. Look at the picture of the cabbage field and tractor on page 23. In the foreground, the cabbages are big and bold, and they get smaller and fainter in the distance. Practice controlling the amount of ink or paint that you transfer to the paper.

▶ *Alternating faint with strong color also makes lovely patterns. Here, three mushrooms were sliced in half to make printing blocks of different sizes, to correspond with the different strength of color.*

SPONGING SKIES

Using a sponge is a kind of printing technique, as it involves transferring paint over and over again from the same "block." It is great for skies and clouds. Experiment with different colors, some printed on top of each other.

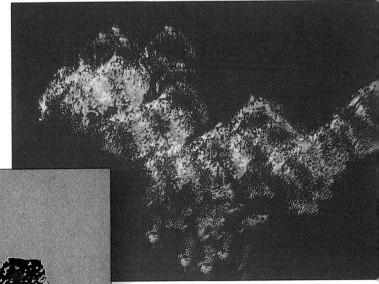

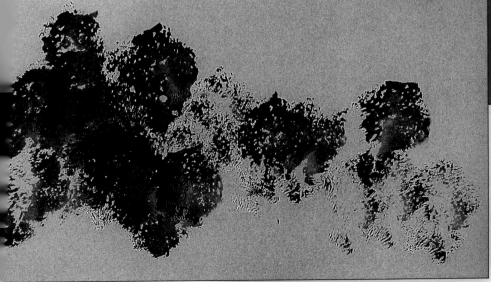

Print the town

WHETHER YOU LIVE IN A CITY, town, or village, you can find exciting shapes and textures in buildings. Dramatic skylines cut from strips of card look wonderful as prints. Walls and roofs can be built up by printing a simple block again and again. The textures of brick and stone can be particularly interesting, so look around to see what you can create.

ROOFS

In many parts of the world, roofs are made from materials found locally.

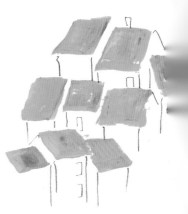

Orangy red paint on cardboard shapes for Mediterranean rooftops

To print a straw-roofed hut – use straw!

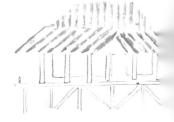

Blocks of corrugated cardboard for corrugated metal roofs.

SUNSET RIVERSIDE

First paint a background of sunset and river. Then make a drawing in the shape of a city skyline on stiff card. With a sharp knife, cut out round the edges of the drawing. Use this card as a block, roll dark paint onto it and press it firmly onto the paper. Then wipe the block clean, and roll a thin layer of paler paint onto the other side. When you press this gently upside down, you've made an exact reflection of the skyline in the river.

WALL PINBOARD

Why not make your own pin pinboard to look like a wall?

Stick wrapping paper onto a pinboard to make a smooth surface (it need not be a single sheet). Make a card block in a brick shape and print a regular pattern over the whole area. Sponge on some gritty patterns to make the wall look rough. When it is dry, coat it with a thin layer of PVA to seal it. Let this dry.

WHAT YOU NEED

Sheet of pinboard to cover

PVA

Paint

Paint brush

Wide glue brush

Card blocks

Sponge

Sandpaper

BRICKWORK

If you want to have brickwork in a picture it is much quicker to print it than to paint it. First paint a background color, and then print blocks of color in a regular pattern.

Brick textures can also be made by wrapping masking tape around a block of cardboard and using it to print.

▲ *Use your pinboard for messages and your favorite photographs. You can write messages or scribble graffiti with a felt-tip pen or chalk — since the surface is sealed with PVA, you can wipe it clean again with a damp sponge. And you can add your own drawings — a mouse is living in this wall!*

Fantastic flowers

Flowers are among the most popular and colorful things to print – they can be whatever you want, realistic or invented. Look around for ideas from dress or furnishing fabrics, and pretty wallpapers. You can even make printed flowers into a pretty bouquet!

▲ *A delicate stenciled tablecloth will enhance any vase of flowers.*

CARDBOARD FLOWERS

These wonderful irises were made by printing with the edges of strips of cardboard.

▶ *Print some flowers, cut them out, and wrap them up in cellophane for a present!*

▲ *Long strips were dipped in thick green paint, and pressed onto paper to make leaf shapes. Blue flowers were made with smaller strips, arranged in a fan shape to make the petals. Yellow and pink dots were added later.*

A PRETTY BOUQUET

You can make bright flowers very easily by melting the wax from crayons. Take care with the hot iron!

1 *Fold a piece of thick paper in half and open it out again. With a vegetable peeler, shave some pieces of wax crayon onto one side of the sheet.*

2 *Fold the paper with the wax inside, and iron over it very gently with a warm iron. The wax will melt into wonderful flower shapes.*

FLOWER TEXTURES

You can get interesting effects by printing through textured material. These speckled petals were made using a piece of net.

RUBBING CRAYON

Rubbing wax crayon gently onto paper with an eraser gives very delicate, smudgy colors.

▲ *Draw flower shapes on stiff paper, and cut out the insides to make stencils. Color round the edges of the shapes with a wax crayon. Then lay the shapes on some drawing paper. With an eraser, rub the crayon color gently onto the paper beneath. The stencils will give clear edges to your flowers.*

Stenciling

EARLY SETTLERS IN NORTH AMERICA could not afford imported wallpaper or decorated furniture. So they printed their own patterns with stencils. This is a wonderfully easy method of making a sharp, clear image — and you can use your stencil again and again. The secret of cutting a stencil is to leave a good width of paper (a "bridge") between the cut-out areas, so that the shapes stay separate when you've inked them.

▲ *You can get striking effects by using gold or silver paint, or stippling little dots of paint from a stiff brush instead of painting solid color.*

A READY-MADE STENCIL

A paper doily makes a good stencil — lay it on a sheet of paper and sponge or brush paint through the holes.

WHAT YOU NEED

Stencil paper or firm drawing paper

Sharp knife

Stencil brush

Pencil

Paints

Sponge

CUTTING A STENCIL

Always make a detailed drawing of your design first, keeping the shapes clear. Don't leave too narrow a strip of paper between the cut-out shapes — it might tear, or your ink or paint might run beneath it. Hold the stencil in place with masking tape at the corners or edges, so that it doesn't slip around.

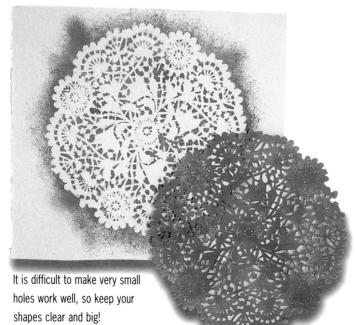

It is difficult to make very small holes work well, so keep your shapes clear and big!

Stenciling is an ideal way to make borders – try one on an old box or some furniture. Or stencil a pattern on a plant pot, fix it with a coat of varnish, and give it as a present.

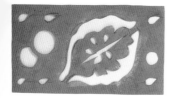

I *Outline the shapes on your stencil paper, using a continuous line with no crossings.*

Light pencil guidelines will keep your borders straight – you can erase them afterwards.

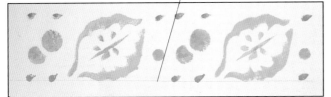

2 *Mix your paints, keeping them fairly dry. Sponge or paint color through the spaces.*

▲ *Fold a square piece of paper four times, then cut a stencil through all the layers. When you open it out, you'll have the same pattern in each section of the sheet.*

▼ *This wonderful multi-colored print was made using a number of stencils.*

▶ *This multi-colored picture has been made using a number of stencils.*

A sponge is good for larger areas.

Use a brush for the smaller shapes.

Make as many eggs as you like!

My word!

STENCILING IS A VERY GOOD WAY of printing neat and tidy letters, which you can arrange into words to make big, bold labels for things. When you make a stencil alphabet, do not throw away the inside shapes of the letters – you can use these as printing blocks. That way you get two whole alphabets at the same time!

ALPHABET STENCILS

You can buy a set of alphabet stencils very cheaply, but it's fun to make your own. Any strong card will do, but special stencil paper is better because you can wipe it clean and use it again and again.

1 Divide a sheet of card into equal sized squares, leaving a space between each square and between each row. Make enough squares for each letter or number you want to print.

2 Draw a letter in each square. Make the shapes clear and solid so they will print boldly.

3 With a craft knife, cut out each shape. This can be difficult, so take care or ask for help. Keep both the stencil letters and the cut-out letter shapes.

50

DECORATED LETTERS

Decorated letters look wonderful. If you cut an elaborate stencil containing decoration, you can use different colors for the different parts. These look really good on folders, boxes, and wrapping paper. Why not make a whole set of writing paper and cards with your own name or initials on?

Print these letters on posters, labels, and wrapping paper.

A decorated letter makes a very special book cover.

You can use letter stencils to make pictures, too!

Stenciled letters personalize this envelope.

The four seasons

T REES CAN LOOK COMPLETELY DIFFERENT with each season of the year. You can use a range of printing methods to decorate one tree shape, to make it change from spring blossom to summer fruit, from fall leaves to bare winter branches. Then put all four together to give you a year-round picture.

Tree printing block

Apple print made from potato block

TREES IN SEASON

Draw a bare tree on a sheet of stiff paper. Cut around the shape and either use the mask as a stencil or the tree as a printing block. Print the tree trunk four times, and decorate each one with images from a season of the year.

SPRING

Roll pale green paint onto some leaves and print them on the branches. Print round pink and white shapes for the blossom — you could use the end of a carrot.

SUMMER

In summer the leaves are darker and apples grow on the branches. Print the leaves a deeper green, and make apples with a potato block dipped in red or green paint — or a mixture of the two.

Snowflake stencils

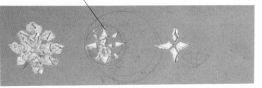

FALL

Trees in the fall are covered with rich golden leaves. Make an explosion of color with orange and red leaf shapes, and let some drop on the ground like golden coins.

WINTER

Paint a darker background for winter, leaving the tree bare. Stencil white snowflakes in the sky. If you like, scatter some glitter on the paint while it is drying to make the snow sparkle.

HANGING PICTURES

Once you have made a series of pictures it's nice to display them in an attractive way.

1 *Stick a length of strong paper to the top of your picture, at the back, so that is sticks up about 6in (15cm). Fold this over to the back and stick just the edge down, leaving a tunnel along the top.*

2 *Cut out squares along the folded edge. Thread a piece of dowelling or thin bamboo through the tunnel, and hang it on the wall with string.*

Cameras and computers

Photographers make their prints in a darkroom by shining a bright light through negative film onto special paper. Computer prints and photocopies are made by an even more complicated process. With these methods it is best to let science do the processing, and you can just have fun with the results.

Snapshot collage

If you have a collection of snapshots or cuttings, you can display them for everyone to enjoy in a collage. Arrange some of your favorite things on a sheet of cardboard. When you're happy with the positions, stick each one down. Look at page 53 for how to make a hanging frame to put your collage on the wall.

Computer art

Perhaps you have worked or played with a computer, and know some of the possibilities of these amazing machines to make extraordinary repeated patterns. If your computer has a color printer, so much the better!

USING A PHOTOCOPIER

A photocopier is a quick way of making many copies of a picture. You can often make your picture larger or smaller, too.

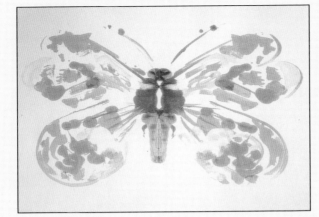

Photocopiers don't just print from flat artwork or paper. This odd shape was made from a photocopy of a crumpled glove — with an eye, some whiskers, and rabbit teeth added!

PRINTING YOUR OWN T-SHIRT

You can print a photocopied picture onto any smooth fabric, such as a T-shirt, pillowcase, or bag. Like lots of printing methods, it will print your picture backwards, like that in a mirror. To get it the right way round, ask for a reverse photocopy to be made. This is most important if you have words or numbers in your image!

WHAT YOU NEED

Photocopy transfer medium (available from craft shops)

Thick brush

T-shirt or fabric

Sponge

Photocopy of your picture

Clean roller

Foil or plastic sheet

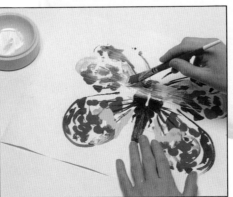

1 *Lay the T-shirt on a flat surface and put a sheet of foil or plastic inside. Brush a layer of the transfer medium onto a photocopy of your picture, then lay it front side down on the fabric. Press firmly with a clean roller and leave to dry.*

2 *After a few hours, peel off the photocopy, and rub away the backing with a sponge. Your printed picture will appear! Paint another coat of the transfer medium on top of the picture and let this dry to seal the print.*

Monoprints

A MONOPRINT IS UNLIKE ANY other print. Its name means "one print" and what you make can never be repeated. A monoprint is made by pressing a piece of paper onto an inked slab. The textures and shapes you can get are impossible to create by painting. They will be unpredictable – sometimes a mess, but sometimes brilliant!

DESIGNING A COCKEREL

Many artists have used the cockerel as an inspiration for paintings or prints. Its proud stance and the texture and patterns of its feathers and skin make it very exciting to draw.

WHAT YOU NEED

Glass or Formica slab, or thick acetate sheet

Water-based printing inks

Paint brush

Paper

Clean roller

Rags

SAFETY NOTE

If you use a glass slab, make sure the edges are smooth or rounded.

1 *Spread printing ink on a glass slab. Use brushes, twigs, and anything that makes an interesting mark to draw an image into the ink. Wipe areas of ink away with a rag. Work quickly and boldly until you have a design you like.*

2 *Lay a sheet of paper over your design. Holding it in position, use your hand or a clean roller to press the paper onto the paint. If you want to add more colors, fix one side of the paper to the slab with sticky tape. Fold the paper back to dry.*

3 *Add different-colored ink to the slab, and lay the paper back down to print again. The fixing tape makes sure it goes back in exactly the same position, which is called "registering."*

re is another way of making a monoprint.

Put colors on the slab in the areas you want them in the finished print.

1 Roll bands of two different colors of printing ink onto one slab at the same time. Place a sheet of fairly thin paper very lightly on top.

2 Draw a design carefully, pressing hard only where you draw. Lift the paper off and you'll see that the colors have printed your design in reverse, with lighter, smudgier colors in the background.

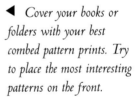

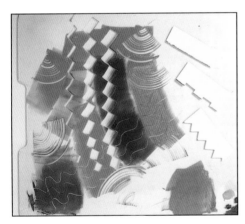

◀ *Cover your books or folders with your best combed pattern prints. Try to place the most interesting patterns on the front.*

▲ *Roll bands of color onto the glass slab. Cut some cardboard combs, scrape patterns into the ink, then take a print. Sometimes the paints merge together and make other colors, sometimes they form thick ridges. The results are always unexpected and exciting.*

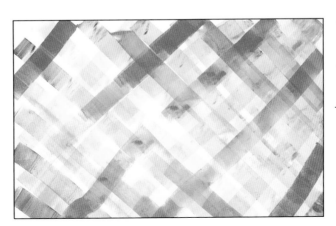

◀ *Don't waste paint when it's time to clean your roller! Roll strips onto a large sheet of paper until the color is faint. Now wipe the roller clean and use it for another color. Do the same again, and you'll have a checkerboard pattern — perfect for wrapping paper.*

Multicolored monoprints

ONOPRINTS CAN PRODUCE SUCH wild, unexpected patterns that you can use them as an exciting starting point, and then draw or print your picture into them. Or make a really wonderful print by building up each color separately, with a drawing under the glass slab as a guide.

PICTURES FROM A MESS!

Perhaps you have printed a real kaleidoscope of mixed-up colors from your slab. Look at it very carefully and you may start to see shapes in it. Try to turn the splodges into plants by adding a few stems and leaves, or make an extraordinary animal by adding some eyes and feet! Maybe it could become an imaginary landscape – an ideal background for a scene of wild beasts or spaceships.

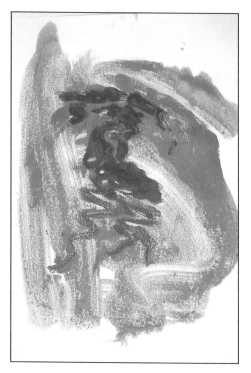

◀ *A wild mixture of paints on the slab makes a colorful, abstract print.*

▶ *With the first print still wet, a second print can be taken off it by pressing paper onto its surface. With the patterns now simplified, the second print will begin to look like something – here, a few lines drawn with a felt-tip pen makes a Spanish dancer!*

A THREE-COLOR PRINT

You can make a more complicated monoprint by building up the color in stages. For this you will need a transparent rolling surface (glass or clear plastic are ideal) so that you can place your sketch underneath as a guide. Tape your paper down on one side to make a hinge, so that it goes back in exactly the same position for each inking.

I *Draw a simple picture on a sheet of paper to act as a guide, and slide it under your glass slab. Put the first color on the slab, in the place where you want it in the picture. Press the paper down carefully and evenly all over. Lift it off and let it dry. Wipe the printing slab clean, and paint in your second color. Take a second print and let it dry again.*

Tape your paper down on one side to keep it in position.

Don't worry about the smudges – they're part of the fun!

2 *Take a third print in the same way. This print is made with three colors — first yellow, then red, then blue — but when you've practiced you can build up even more. Some of your inks will probably print over each other at the edges. This is called "overprinting" and it isn't necessarily a mistake — many printers do it on purpose to make even more colors out of the mixtures.*

▲ *If the ink on your monoprint is really thick, you can lay a sheet of paper on top and make a paler print of your print! It will be reversed.*

59

Lino cuts

For about a hundred years linoleum has been used to make prints. It was a new material – made from cork and oil – that was used for flooring. It is ideal for detailed cutting and will allow prints to be taken from it again and again, so it has been used by printers ever since. It is a wonderful material to work with – and it even smells pleasant!

CUTTING TIPS

• Special lino tools are very sharp, so practice first to get the feel of them, and find out what marks each tool makes. Always keep both hands behind the blade so that you don't risk cutting yourself.

• Place your block with the top edge against something firm, such as a wall, so it won't slip. This makes cutting much easier.

• Cut away enough background, but make the cuts shallow. Deep cutting will break the string backing of the lino.

• Remember that what you cut away will not print, and will therefore be white in your picture.

CUTTING A PATTERN

You can buy lino, or use a thick vinyl floor tile. A sharp craft knife will do for simple shapes, but you may want to buy special tools (you can get them at most art shops). It is a good idea to warm the lino before starting – it makes cutting easier.

CUTTING THE BLOCK

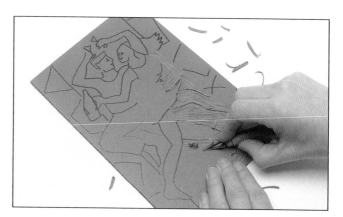

1 *Draw your design on a piece of lino. Cut away the areas and lines you don't want to print.*

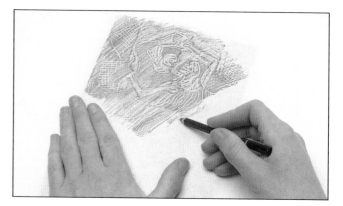

2 *To check what your print will look like, lay a sheet of thin paper over the block and rub all over with a soft pencil. You can still make changes!*

3 *Spread ink on your inking slab and roll your roller over it to get a good coating of ink. Roll it evenly over the lino block.*

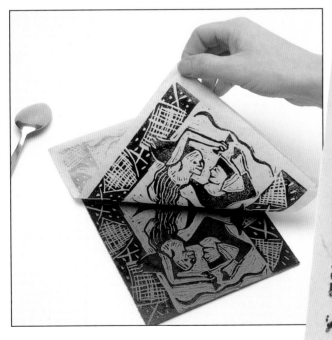

4 *Lay your paper on top of the inked surface. Smooth it down with your fingers so there are no air bubbles underneath. Roll all over it with a clean roller.*

PAPER TIPS

Try printing the same lino cut on different kinds of paper – colored paper, tracing paper, brown wrapping paper, or tissue paper – and see the differences. The thinner the paper, the more detail you'll get – but don't go too thin, or it might tear.

5 *Peel the paper off carefully, starting with one corner, then leave it to dry. When it is quite dry, you can display it or frame it.*

Colored lino cuts

NOW YOU HAVE GOT THE BASIC idea of lino cutting (and, with luck, not too many plasters on your fingers!), why not try some more complicated prints. Here are two ways of making multicolored prints from one block.

WHAT YOU NEED
....

Glass slab
Lino block
Water-based printing inks
Paper
Roller

CUTTING AWAY TO COLOR

This exciting way of making a colored lino print is called a "reduction" print, because after printing each stage you cut more lino away. Sometimes there is very little left on the block by the end! The Spanish artist Picasso loved using this method – and made some wonderfully bold and vigorous prints.

GETTING IT IN REGISTER
When you're making several prints to build up lots of colors, you must keep the paper in exactly the same place on the block every time. An easy way to do this is to draw a fine pencil line on your paper round the block. At each stage replace the block exactly inside this outline – but don't do it upside down!

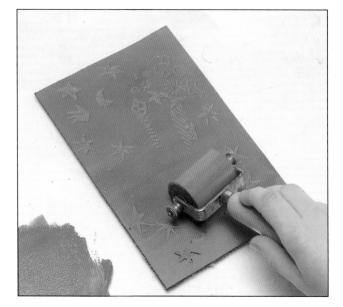

1 First, plan your drawing – this clown print is in red, blue, and turquoise. Cut away the areas you want to leave white, then roll the block evenly with red ink. Take a print and let it dry. Clean the block, then cut away the areas you want to keep red.

2 Roll turquoise ink onto the block and take another print. Remember to place your printing paper in exactly the same place every time. Clean the block again, and this time cut away the areas you want to keep turquoise. Roll the block finally with blue ink, and take the final print.

A JIGSAW PRINT

Here is another way to make a colored print. With a craft knife, cut a lino block right through into a number of shapes, rather like a simple jigsaw puzzle. Roll different-colored ink onto each piece, and reassemble the puzzle, fitting the pieces closely together. Then take a print.

Roll each piece in a different color.

The white lines where the pieces were fitted back together show up the pattern.

Folding the paper in a concertina shape before printing gives you a wonderful pattern.

3 *Lift off the finished print carefully. The final printing of blue ink has gone on top of the other two colors, so they only show through in certain places. The patterns of color are wonderful.*

Lino cut experiments

IF YOU HAVE A LINO BLOCK WITH AN image you really like, you can print it in lots of different ways. A lino block is strong enough to be printed again and again. Try printing different colors on top of each other, printing on folded paper, or onto a tissue paper collage. If you have made a monoprint with swirly colors (look at page 59), print your lino cut on top of this and you will have a masterpiece!

Sharp lino prints look great on top of swirly monoprints.

A collage of colored tissue paper makes a brilliant background.

Print some horses fainter so they look far away.

Overlapping some horses makes them look very realistic.

LITTLE "STAINED GLASS" WINDOWS

The strong printing you get from a black lino cut is a good contrast to colors. Here, a lino-cut print on thick tracing paper gives you the bars in the glass – fill in the spaces with your brightest felt-tip pens. Hang the medallions in front of a window so the light shines through them.

MAKING BAGS FOR PRESENTS

Collect paper bags in different sizes and colors, print them with your horse lino cuts, and tie them with matching ribbons. You can add cards and wrapping paper to your "designer" collection.

Cut a rubber horseshoe stamp to print hoofprints.

SAME BLOCKS — DIFFERENT COLORS

Two blocks — each of a galloping horse — are printed over and over again in different colors on a big sheet of paper. A stampede like this would make a dramatic frieze for your room!

65

Signed and sealed

SEALS WERE AMONG THE EARLIEST FORMS of printing and have been used for many thousands of years. A pattern is pressed into warm wax – when the wax cools and hardens, the image is perfectly preserved. Seals can be simple or very ornate; they can be carved onto the ends of wooden knobs, or form part of beautiful jewelry – "signet" rings are those with seals on, for signing letters. Taking shapes in wax or plaster is used for many things – from impressions for false teeth to masks for the theater!

SEALS OF OLD

Both paper and printing were invented in Northern China, many centuries ago. Chinese nobles had small wooden blocks specially carved with their name or mark, which were dipped in paints made from soot or earth, and stamped onto paper or fabric. Because such seals are hard to forge, they are an important way of showing that something is real and not a copy. Rulers used them to issue laws, and artists to authenticate their work.

SIMPLE SEALS

Shells, coins, buttons, nuts, bolts, and paper clips all make good impressions in wax.

Corks

Things to stick on the corks

This letter has been sealed with little scraps of dried flowers and leaves, pressed into melted wax.

Sealing wax

The seal used here was made by arranging three little hooks in a pattern.

SEALED LETTERS

Before the days of gummed envelopes, letters were folded and sealed. If the seal was broken, you knew someone had looked inside! You can either make a seal from sealing wax or use a colored candle.

WHAT YOU NEED

Sealing wax or colored candle wax

Things to press into the wax

Corks to make mounts

Glue

Envelopes, paper, ribbon, string, etc.

To make your own old-looking document, tear a piece
thick paper to give rough edges, and stain it with tea.
ow it's ready for you to write an important
ocument! Roll it up loosely and fix it
ith a ribbon and seal.

▲ *Melt some candle wax to make a thick*
blob. When it is almost dry, drop on more
wax to make the blob thicker. Wait until it
looks cloudy, and then press a seal firmly
into the wax lump.

PLASTER OF PARIS IMPRESSIONS

Sometimes a kind of light plaster , known as plaster of Paris, is
used to make shapes. For this theater mask, quick-drying rubber
was smoothed over the actor's face. When it is peeled off, plaster
is poured into the shape. This sets to make an exact copy of the
face, and is used to build a mask which will fit perfectly.

Plaster mold from which the
mask will be made
in a perfect fit.

◄ *This half-mask was made for a fairy in "A Midsummer Night's*
Dream", a play by William Shakespeare. A papier mache shell was
molded round the plaster mask, then painted in delicate colors.

Lasting impressions

LAYING DAMP PAPER OVER different bumps and shapes leaves a permanent impression when the paper dries. This technique can make interesting three-dimensional backgrounds for your pictures, because you can indicate shapes without using any color or lines.

BRAILLE WRITING

Braille is a system of reading for the blind invented nearly two hundred years ago. Patterns of raised dots represent letters, and people read books by running their fingers over the bumps. It was used by the French general Napoleon to pass silent messages among his soldiers so the enemy wouldn't hear them.

▲ *Braille letters take up a lot of space, so books are enormous. You could invent a simple form of braille and use it as a special code among your friends.*

PAPER IMPRESSIONS

The patterns in your paper will come out better if you press the shapes into the paper under a really heavy weight. A printing press is ideal.

◄ *Arrange torn paper and card so that there are several levels, but the surface is fairly flat. Dampen a sheet of heavy paper, lay it on top, weight it, and leave it overnight to dry. You will have a different pattern on each side. Complete a picture by painting, or adding colored stencils or stamps.*

DOUBLE YOUR MONEY!

Make a fairly flat pile of coins. Cover them with a piece of foil, and gently press it onto the pile. Rub the surfaces gently with your fingers through the foil, taking care not to tear it. Soon you'll have an extra pile of silver money!

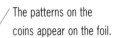

The patterns on the coins appear on the foil.

A TREASURE CHEST FOR YOUR MONEY

If you possess a sturdy box, you can easily turn it into a very special money-box. First cut a neat slit in the top. Spread a thin layer of glue all over the box, and press on lots of small coins and money symbols cut out of thick card. Then cut a large sheet of silver foil and wrap the box completely, pressing it in to show up the shapes. If you rub in some dark ink, it will make the foil look old, and adding gold touches will make it look like it is made of precious metal.

Money symbols cut from thick card.

Rubbings

MAKING RUBBINGS CAN REALLY FEEL like magic. When you lay a piece of blank paper over a textured object, and rub over it with a crayon or soft pencil, you see a pattern literally appearing before your eyes. Some wonderful rubbings can be made from gravestones in churchyards, but you can make exciting pictures from the simplest things, such as stones or leaves.

▲ *Try making a rubbing from stone, as here, or brick or tree bark with a soft wax crayon in a range of bright colors.*

CHURCHYARD RUBBINGS

Many churchyards contain decorated memorials, sometimes very old and beautiful. To make a really good rubbing, it is worth buying the right materials from an art shop. These include a special sort of wax, which is perfect for bringing out all the details. It is not expensive, and you can get it in many different colors.

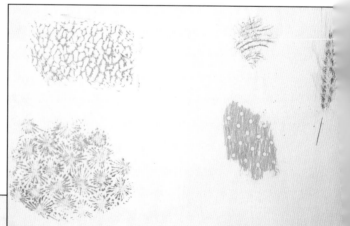

Old window glass sometimes makes good patterns. Tape a sheet of thin paper over the patterned side, and rub with a dark-colored wax crayon.

▲ *Collage blocks — like the string block made on page 35 — make interesting surfaces to rub. Cover the block with a sheet of thin paper, rub it gently with candle wax, and then stain it with thin paint.*

Delicate rubbings from feathers.

Leaves make very good rubbings.

▲ *Collect leaves from a garden or park, and make rubbings with different-colored crayons, or candle wax and stains made with thin paint.*

71

Etching and scratching

SOME METHODS OF PRINTING ARE QUITE DANGEROUS. Etchings are made when strong chemicals eat away lines and patterns in metal – the strong fumes mean that etchers usually wear masks and use ventilators. It is something to try if you ever go to art college, but meanwhile you can try something similar by scratching marks onto Perspex and printing them like an etching. This is called drypoint.

Smooth-ended tool for rubbing

Fine scratchi

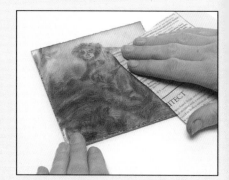

Roller

Colored wax

WHAT YOU NEED

Sheet of Perspex or thick plastic

Tools with sharp points, such as a compass or 6in nail

Ink and roller

Old rags

Soft paper for printing

Newspaper

▲ *The famous seventeenth-century Dutch painter Rembrandt was a superb etcher. Look at how the finest lines came out beautifully in his etching of the Holy Family on the flight into Egypt.*

SCRATCHING INTO PERSPEX

1 *Plan your drawing first, then cover the sheet of plastic with a thin layer of wax. This will enable you to see the marks you scratch. Try to make the marks varied – crisscrossing, deeper or thicker cuts, dots, lines, and dashes. Wipe off the wax and rub ink all over it with a soft rag, pressing it well into the grooves.*

2 *Wipe all the ink off the surface with a piece of folded newspaper held flat. This removes ink only from the surface, because you want to leave all the ink in the grooves.*

ETCHING WITH A PRESS

◀ *Here is the etching taken from the metal plate. This way of printing allows you to make lines as fine as a hair, or a large block of thick ink. It's a good method for cartoon pictures such as this one.*

This metal plate has been etched with strong chemicals to leave deep grooves. Ink is pressed into these grooves, and smoothed off the shiny surface. A sheet of damp paper is placed on the plate, and the two are put through a heavy press where the ink is squeezed onto the paper.

Dampened paper brings out more ink.

Use colored inks to get different effects.

Silk-screen printing

SILK-SCREEN PRINTING IS A METHOD in which ink is squeezed through a fine mesh screen onto a surface, leaving areas that are masked off unprinted. The result is a pattern of inked and blank shapes. The screen is very fine, so the ink goes onto the paper in a very solid, strong block, with the edges of the pattern clear and crisp.

◀ *Medieval knights wore colored crosses on their tunics. These were early silk-screens, printed by blocking out a cross on a fine fabric screen with pitch or tar, then pressing paint through the mesh.*

MAKING YOUR OWN SCREEN

If you do not want to buy a silk-screen from an art shop, you can build your own, or get someone to do it for you. You can adapt an old picture frame, but the best frame for stretching the mesh is a rectangle made of 1in (2.5cm) wood. Old net curtain makes a very good mesh screen – make sure it is completely plain.

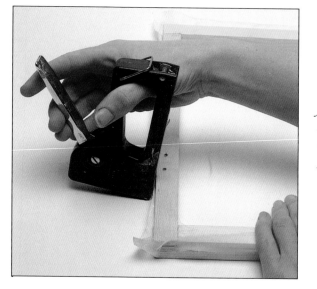

1 *Make the frame whatever size you want. Wet the net and wring it out so it is evenly damp. Stretch it over the frame as tightly as possible, and secure it all round with a staple gun.*

WHAT YOU NEED

Wooden frame
Nylon net or muslin
Staple gun
Gum strip
Waterproof PVA medium or varnish

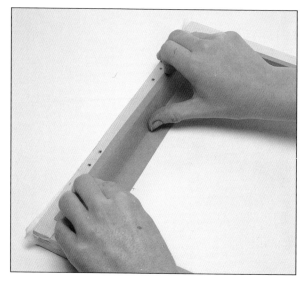

2 *Turn the frame over so the mesh is underneath. Stick gum strip all round the inside edge, so the mesh is joined to the frame. Turn it back over, and stick more gum strip all round to match the first strip. When the strips are dry, paint on PVA medium or varnish to make them waterproof. The whole screen will tighten when it is dry.*

TORN PAPER PRINT

WHAT YOU NEED

Silk-screen

Screen printing inks

Thin paper

Squeegee (available from craft shops)

Printing paper

Squeegee should be slightly narrower than screen.

1 Put a large sheet of printing paper on a hard, flat base. Arrange torn strips of paper in a pattern on top. Place the screen squarely over this stencil. Pour ink onto the top end of the screen and pull evenly with a squeegee down the surface of the screen, pressing the ink well in. This is easier if you get someone else to hold the screen while you ink.

2 The squeegee forces the ink through the screen onto the paper. It also makes the stencil stick to the screen, so that you can make several prints with the same pattern.

SCREEN-PRINTING INKS

Most craft shops sell a special screen-printing medium. You mix it with gouache or acrylic paints to make a thick waterproof ink, which is an ideal texture for screen-printing.

▶ If you put blue ink on the left side of the screen, and yellow on the right, they will mix at the edges when pulled across the mesh, making a stripe of green in the middle.

75

Multicolored screen-printing

A PRINTING SCREEN CAN BE USED over and over again. Water-based inks can be rinsed off under a tap, and then you can start again with another color or design. For complicated color prints, you will need help with holding the screen steady. If you can, get someone who is good at woodwork to make you a hinge to hold the screen up which makes printing easier.

A piece of hardboard attached to the bottom of the screen will enable you to make guidelines and keep your print in register.

PRINTING A TWO-COLOR STENCIL

You can easily build up colored stencils in stages. Draw a simple design and decide at the beginning where you want each color – this is important! Trace the picture and cut out the area to be printed. All the green areas on this stencil have been cut out first. Take the first print – it's a good idea to mark the position of the corners on the frame with sticky tape, so that you get the paper back in exactly the same place for each color.

Attach two pegs with hinges, so that you can prop your screen up.

Sticky tape to mark the corners will keep the print in register.

I When you've printed the first color, trace the areas for the second color (here it is orange) from the design onto a sheet of tracing paper and cut out these spaces. Replace the print on the bed, and place the second stencil on top so the spaces are where you want the orange ink to go.

Flat, thick color and clean edges are typical of screen-prints.

USING THE REMAINS

You will have some strange shapes left over after cutting the stencils. Try sticking them on a clean screen, and making another print. You may have some surprises!

2 *Lay the screen on top and pull some orange ink across the mesh with the squeegee. Lift off the print and leave it to dry. When you get good at this, you can add as many colors as you like.*

Fabric printing

PRINTING YOUR OWN DESIGN IS very exciting if you can then wear it! Most of the printing you have tried so far has been on paper, but you can also make prints on fabric, foil, or even plastic. Repeat your print along a length of fabric, and you have made your own dressmaking material. You can also print T-shirts with individual patterns.

WHAT YOU CAN PRINT ON

Fabric for printing needs to be fairly fine weave — this makes the design clearer. New fabric should be washed first to soften it and allow it shrink. Old net curtains and gauze make excellent printing materials.

Heart stencil for printing

As you repeat the printing, the colors will fade.

PRINTING FABRIC

Cut heart shapes out of a large sheet of tracing paper or newspaper to make a stencil. Lay the fabric smoothly on the base of the frame, cover with the stencil, close the screen, and pour printing ink across the top of the screen. Pull this firmly down the mesh with a squeegee. Keep moving the fabric along in the frame to repeat the pattern down its length.

▲ *Printing a T-shirt is very easy and looks marvelous. This one has been printed with the torn paper stencil shown on page 75. Put a sheet of card inside the T-shirt so that the fabric stays taut and print in exactly the same way as on paper.*

You can draw directly onto the mesh screen with water-based crayons (they'll wash off afterwards). Then, instead of ink or paint, you press wallpaper paste through the screen with the squeegee. The paste dissolves the crayon colors through the screen onto the paper beneath. This is almost like doing a painting, but the screen mesh gives the areas of paint a texture like fabric. You can get beautiful effects with sweeps of mixed color, and areas of fine detail.

1 First draw your picture directly onto the mesh screen.

2 Use lots of different bright colors to get the best effect.

3 Mix wallpaper paste till it's creamy, and press it through the mesh.

4 Lift up the screen and remove the picture carefully.

Fancy dress

PRINTING ALLOWS YOU TO MAKE wonderful things very quickly and often cheaply. You can cover large areas of paper or fabric at great speed, and create exotic costumes for yourself and your friends, so it's great for dressing up. If you use old materials, you do not have to worry that they will not last — just make more!

"The Queen of Hearts, she made some tarts . . ." You can print all you need for this costume, and finish it with a decorated crown.

Crown made from cardboard, covered in foil, and decorated with hearts.

Jam tarts printed with potato blocks.

▲ *Make a pinafore with printed heart material — an old sheet would be ideal.*

80

...pirate costume is easy to put together — old trousers ...d a shirt, wellington boots and a colored scarf. But ...ow about making a brilliant parrot to sit on your

shoulder, a skull-and-crossbones flag, and an old map showing how to find the hidden treasure?

▲ *Look at page 28 for how to print feathers. Draw the outline of a parrot on a piece of card and fill it with brightly colored feather prints. Add details with felt-tip pens and attach wire to the back with tape, so it can sit on your shoulder.*

▲ *Draw a map of hidden treasure on a sheet of torn paper stained with tea to look old, and close it with a seal. Page 67 shows you how to do this.*

Lithography

ONE METHOD OF PRINTING USED by some famous artists is lithography, which means "drawing on stone." It is said to have been invented hundreds of years ago by a playwright who scribbled his laundry list on a stone, then found the image had printed in reverse onto some clothes. The modern version of this is called photolithography – inked images are put onto a huge roller and then transferred to the paper. This means that the image can be printed the right way round.

▲ *Modern four-color printing machines – such as the one shown here – give very fine adjustments to how strong the inks will be. Someone must still check the prints, however!*

LITHOGRAPHY – HOW SEPARATE COLORS ARE PUT TOGETHER

A lithograph is made by drawing or painting with greasy ink on a metal plate. This then goes through lots of processes, so that the printing ink will stick to the drawn areas and wash off all the rest. A heavy roller passes over the inked plate, and transfers the inky picture onto a sheet of paper. There has to be a separate plate for each color – it could be as many as 12. All the different colors – together with any new colors made by blendings – build up to make the finished picture.

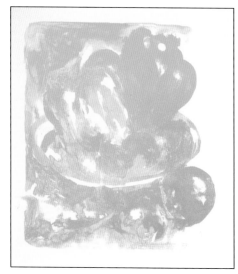

The main background color is printed first.

The red plate is printed next.

The green plate is printed last.

82

◀ This lithograph of cows in a field was made from separate color plates. Where they have overlapped and printed on top of each other, they make even more colors. Lithographs often have a very attractive soft texture.

Repeats of the same pattern can look great when built up with different colors.

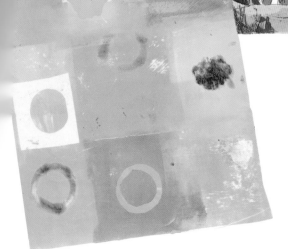

▶ The French painter Toulouse-Lautrec loved lithography. How many different colors can you count in his image called "The Jockey"?

◀ This lithograph of peppers and tomatoes was made from three color plates. Look how the three colors mix together to make different shades of brown for the shadows. This mixing to make new colors is one of the exciting things about multicolored printing - you never quite know what's going to happen!

PRINTING WITH A PRESS

Most serious printers use a press to make their prints. This puts an enormous amount of pressure onto the printing block, so that even the most delicate marks, textures, and patterns are squeezed onto the paper.

Experiment with your prints by using different amounts of pressure, then compare the results.

Wood works

ALL PRINTING USED TO BE DONE with wood – some of the most beautiful illustrations in old books were made from wooden blocks carved in the most intricate detail. In some countries they still use wood blocks for printing on fabric. You can cut very fine lines on wood, and make its grainy texture part of the pattern.

▲ *Thomas Bewick was a remarkable wood engraver who lived 300 years ago in England. He illustrated many books with pictures of animals and birds. He used a very hard wood called boxwood for his prints – one of his printing blocks was used 900,000 times!*

WHAT YOU NEED

Piece of balsa wood

Tools, such as a knife, knitting needle, etc.

Inked slab

Rollers

Paper

MAKING A WOOD BLOCK

Because it lasts so well, a wood block is a good choice for a design you want to keep and use over and over again. So it's worth taking care to get it right – make practice sketches before you finalize your design.

▲ *When you're happy with your design, cut round the edges with a sharp knife. You could also press lines in the wood with a knitting needle.*

Remember that the finished image will print in reverse.

The block needs plenty of ink, as wood is absorbent.

These sharp
wood-cut fish look
marvelous printed
bright colors.

Different effects are made by
alternating dark and light colors
for ink and paper.

▲ This wood block
comes from India.
It is traditionally used
to stamp a repeated pattern
across a width of cloth, and
would last for many years.

Living in print

Now you have tried lots of ways of printing, you could combine different methods to decorate your room in a very special way. It will not cost a lot, so you can easily change it when you want to try out new ideas.

Decorate your room

Bedroom, classroom, den – anywhere that needs a bit of livening up can be transformed by your printing efforts. Here are just a few ideas: stenciled or printed floors or furniture; printed bedclothes, cushions, or curtains; folders and books covered with marbled paper; leaf prints on walls; prints on mirrors and windows.

▲ *See how good the lino-cut horse (from page 64) looks when it is printed on wood. The grain showing through adds to its effect. If you find a piece of unpainted wood no one wants, print a group of horses galloping along it.*

Stars at night

Invisible in the light, luminous paint comes to life after dark. If you can get permission, try decorating the ceiling of your room with moons and stars glowing in a deep blue sky!

What you need

Luminous paint
Paint brush
Printing blocks
A firm ladder
Someone to help you!

Make card printing blocks of planets, stars, moons, and rockets. Plan your design carefully, then print the blocks on the ceiling using luminous paint. Wait until dark!

SPECIAL BOXES

Do not throw away prints you dislike or consider failures — they can often be useful. You can make a colorful set of storage boxes in different sizes, by using shoe boxes, chocolate boxes, and anything else you can find. Transform them with a patchwork of printed paper. Seal them with varnish or diluted PVA medium and they will last a long time.

▲ *Here is a special box for your diary or other secret things. It is covered with foil imprinted with the shape of a question mark. You could mark your other boxes with secret signs that only you will understand.*

▶ *You can make lovely frames for your best prints — and your favorite photos and treasures — from cardboard stuck with shapes and covered with inked foil.*

MORE IDEAS

• Keep one print from all your blocks, stamps, and other techniques in a special book or folder. Even when they have worn out or been thrown away, you'll still have a record of every one.
• Use stencils to make a pattern on a plain lampshade, or stencil narrow strips of paper to make a frieze round a window or door.
• Print your name on your door using your set of stenciled letters.

Print celebrations

FESTIVALS AND CELEBRATIONS ARE A great opportunity to use your printing skills. Printing allows you to make things in quantity, like sets of Christmas cards or party invitations. And once you have a shape or an image you really like, you can make prints on lots of things. A themed party is easy this way!

Gold holly stencils make red balloons look Christmassy

PARTIES

Print invitations, paper plates, and mugs (waterproof paint only!). Decorate balloons with glitter paint shapes – blow up a balloon, print a shape on it using glue, and sprinkle glitter over it. Print a line of rubber stamp prints as a decoration for thank-you letters, and close them with a personal seal.

FEASTS AND HOLIDAYS

Christmas and other big feasts are a chance to go wild and fill the house with printed decorations. You can make paper chains – print sheets of colored paper with gold stars, cut them into equal strips, and make them into a chain. For Easter, paint some blown eggs and decorate them with tiny rubber stamp designs.

Holly stencils can be made into a paper chain.

People always love receiving handmade presents — and you can wrap them in hand-patterned paper and add your own handmade cards, too.

◀ *This picture frame is made with printed feathers and rubber stamp diamonds. The image inside is a silk-screen Christmas tree which you can put on matching wrapping paper.*

Use favorite silk-screen stencils for cards, papers, crackers, and bags.

A range of papers with matching prints in different colors.

Finishing work

THE VERY BEST PRINTERS ARE THOSE WHO clean up after work, put tops on paints, wash brushes, clean surfaces and tools, and store work safely. Can you imagine what the very worst are like? If you store your prints carefully you will have a collection of wonderful things to use now and lots of fun later!

MAKING A SCRAP
BOOK OR FOLDER

Use stiff cardboard to make the folder and cover it with paper. Stick a favorite print on the front, or decorate the whole cover with a pattern of rubber stamps. Attach some tape or ribbon to close the folder, and fill it with your best work.

> WHAT YOU NEED
> ....
> Large sheet of paper
> Two sheets of cardboard
> the same size
> Tape or ribbon
> Glue

▲ *Keep your best prints to mount on colored card, either to display, or to send to friends.*

DRYING PRINTS

In printers' studios you will often see a row of prints hanging up to dry in a special rack. But you can easily dry prints by hanging them to some string with clothes pegs. You might find a print is bumpy and crinkled. Don't worry – lay it under a flat board with some heavy weights on top for a couple of hours.

USING PRINTS YOU DON'T LIKE

Don't throw away any failures. Cut them up into small shapes and glue them onto a big sheet of paper to make "patchwork" paper. You can use this to cover boxes, make a screen, or wrap presents.

FAMOUS PRINTERS

Now you know a little bit about printing, you may enjoy seeing prints in museums and galleries, and come away with lots of good ideas. Many museums have special print rooms but you might have to get special permission to visit them. Some museums have special exhibitions of printing.

Famous artists who were specially interested in printmaking include Albrecht Dürer in the fifteenth century, Rembrandt in the seventeenth century, Toulouse-Lautrec in the nineteenth century, and Henri Matisse, Edvard Munch, Pablo Picasso, and Andy Warhol in the twentieth century. Have a look at their work in books – it may give you some ideas.

Index

Page numbers in *italic* refer to
illustrations or captions on
those pages.

A
animal footprints 32, *32-3*
ant prints *33*
apple prints 18, *18*, 25

B
backgrounds 42, *42-3*
  colored paper 37, *37*
bags 65, *65*
bees, fingerprint 14, *14*
"Birds in a Birdbath" 28, *28*
bleach, printing with 38, *38-9*, *39*
blocks, lino-cut *60-1*
blotting paper *12*
boats *22-3*
books:
  covers *21*
  flickbooks 31, *31*
bouquets *46*
"A Box of Beasts" 33, *33*
boxes, decorating *87*
Braille 68, *68*
brickwork *45*
bubble prints 24, *24*
buildings 44, *44-5*
burnishing 13
butterflies, potato-print 16, *16-17*
buttons *24*

C
card *12*
cardboard:
  corrugated 22, *22-3*
  flowers 46, *46*
carrier bags 29, *29*

cat footprints *32*
cauliflower prints *37*
Christmas 88
churchyard rubbings 70, *70*
cockerels *56*
coins 69, *69*
collage 64
  corrugated cardboard *22-3*
  photographs 54, *54*
  printing from 20, *20-1*
  rubbings *71*
colored paper backgrounds 37, *37*
computer prints 54, *54*
corn stalks *26*
corrugated cardboard *12*, 22, *22-3*
crayons 47, *47*

D
disappearing ink 38, *38-9*
distance effects 43
doilies *20*
dolls' houses *31*
"Double Your Money" 69, *69*
drawing paper *12*
drying prints 91

E
"Edible Patterns" 35
equipment *12*, *12*, 13, *13*
etching 72, *72-3*

F
fabric printing 78, *78-9*
fancy dress 80, *80-1*
feathers 28, *28*, *71*
ferns 29, *29*
"Fingerprint Bees" 14, *14*
fingerprints 14
fish *85*

fleas 31, *31*
flick books 31, *31*
flowers 46, *46-7*
folders 90, *90*
food, prints of 25
footprints 15, *15*
  animals 32, *32-3*
frames, picture 30, *39*, 89
friezes, leaf-pattern 27, *27*
fronds 28, *28-9*
fruit prints 18, *18-19*

G
"A Gathering Storm" 22
glue blocks 21, *21*
"A Goldfish Pond" 41, *41*
"Grand Canyon" 36, *36*
"Greengrocer's Stall" *19*

H
handles 22
hanging pictures 53, *53*
horseshoes *32*

I
impressing paper 68, *68-9*
inking rollers *12*
inks 13
  disappearing 38, *38-9*
  screen printing 75

J
jigsaw prints *63*
"Jumping Fleas" 31, *31*

L
landscape prints 36, *36-7*

ndscape backgrounds 42, *42-3*
af prints 26, *26*
aves *71*
ttering:
  decorated *51*
  stencils 50, *50-1*
ino *12*
ino cuts 60, *60-1*
  colored 62, *62-3*
  experiments 64, *64-5*
lip prints 15, *15*
lithography 82, *82-3*

M

manuscripts 10, *10*
marbling 40, *40-1*
masks *67*
materials 12, *12*, 13, *13*
money 69, *69*
monoprints 56, *56-7*
  multicolored 58, *58-9*
mouse prints *33*
multicolored prints:
  linocuts 62, *62-3*
  lithography 82, *82-3*
  monoprints 58, *58-9*
  silk-screen 76, *76-7*

N

nature prints 26, *26-7*
  seasons 52, *52-3*

P

paints *13*
paper *12*
  colored 37, *37*
  marbled 40, *40-1*
paper doilies *20*
parties *88*
perspex, scratching *72-3*
photocopies 54, *55*
photographs 54, *54-5*

picture:
  frames 39, *39*, 89
  hanging 53, *53*
pinboards 45, *45*
"Pirate" *80*
plaster of Paris 67, *67*
poster paint *13*
potato prints 16, *16-17*
presses 10, *10*
printing, basic 11, *11*
printing block handles *22*
printing presses 10, *10*
  etching *73*
  lithography *83*
prints, drying *91*
puzzle cards 24, *24*

Q

"Queen of Hearts" *80*

R

rollers *12*
roofs *44*
rooms, decorating 86, *86-7*
rubber stamps:
  making 30, *30*
  using 30, *30-1*
rubbings 70, *70-1*

S

safety 13, *39*, 56
scrap books 90, *90*
scratching 72, *72-3*
screen printing 74, *74-5*
  fabrics *78-9*
  multicolored 76, *76-7*
seals 66, *66-7*
seasons 52, *52-3*
seed pods *26*
shoe prints 15, *15*
silk-screen printing 74, *74-5*
  fabrics 78, *78-9*

multicolored 76, *76-7*
skeleton leaves *26*
skies 43, *43*
sponging 43, *43*
stained-glass windows 65, *65*
stamps, rubber 30, *30-1*
"Stars at Night" *86*
stenciling 48, *48-9*
  cutting stencils 48, *48*
  ideas for *49*
  lettering 50, *50-1*
  paper *12*
string prints 34, *34-5*
"Sunset Riverside" 44, *44*

T

tissue paper *64*
toast prints 35, *35*
tools 12, *12*, 13, *13*
torn-paper prints *75*
townscapes 44, *44-5*
treasure chest 69, *69*
trees 52, *52-3*
T-shirts 55, *55*
tyre marks *10*

V

vegetable prints *18-19*

W

wire prints 34, *35*
wood blocks 84, *84-5*
wrapping paper *12*, 89
  apple-patterned *18*

Z

zebras *23*